THE AGE OF AI

THE AGE OF AI

AN INTRODUCTION TO BIG DATA, MACHINE LEARNING, AND NEURAL NETWORKS

Marc Stanford

THE AGE OF AI

Copyright© 2020 by Aculeatus Limited
All Rights Reserved

MARC STANFORD
amazon.com/author/marcstanford

Printed in the United States of America
First Printing: February 2020
ISBN-13: 9781705603291

Imprint: Independently published
Cover designed by pro_ebookcovers, FL, USA

No parts of this book may be reproduced, duplicated or transmitted in any form or by any means, electronic or mechanical, including photocopies, recordings or any support without the written permission of the author or publisher. The only exception is by a reviewer, who may quote short excerpts in a review.

All the methods shown in the book are for educational purposes only. The author assumes no responsibility for the improper use of the techniques shown. Under no circumstances will any blame or legal responsibility be held against the publisher, or author, for any damages, reparation, or monetary loss due to the information contained within this book. Either directly or indirectly.

This copyright-protected book is for personal use only. To amend, sell, distribute, use or quote any part, or the content within this book, without the consent of the author or publisher, is not permitted.

This book is dedicated to Dr. John Vincent Atanasoff,
who invented the first computer back in 1937.

CONTENTS

INTRODUCTION	1
ARTIFICIAL INTELLIGENCE	2
MACHINE LEARNING	5
NEURAL NETWORKS	8
RECURRENT NEURAL NETWORKS	13
DEEP LEARNING	15
TENSORFLOW	20
REINFORCEMENT LEARNING	23
Q_LEARNING	26
DATA MINING	29
BIG DATA	33
CONCLUSIONS	37
Appendix: Installation of Anaconda	38
ABOUT THE AUTHOR	39

"The true delight is in the finding out rather than in the knowing."
-*Isaac Asimov*

INTRODUCTION

Artificial Intelligence (AI) is the simulation of the highly complex human intelligence processes by machines, especially computer systems. These processes include learning, reasoning, and self-correction. When presented with an unfamiliar task, a strong AI system can find a solution without human intervention.

Very soon, you can expect Artificial Intelligence and Machine Learning to be part of any form of technology that integrates data exchange and analytics. This impact will continue to grow; AI will transform the Internet and the global economy. The opportunities this prospect creates are enormous, from new services and breakthroughs in science to the growth of human intelligence and convergence with the digital world.

"The Age of AI" is written for readers who like to acquire fundamental knowledge about Artificial Intelligence, Neural Networks, Machine Learning, Deep Learning, Data Mining and Big Data Processing. This book is focused on descriptions of main concepts, principal algorithms and their use as applications in the various fields of AI. It will enable you to gain insight into all essential aspects and significant building blocks of AI consisting of systems with generalized human cognitive abilities.

Today, Artificial Intelligence is widely used in several vital applications of daily life, and you might not yet be consciously aware of it. Still, we are already living in the Age of AI. It's not hard to predict, that in coming years we will enjoy incredible benefits in a world where AI will help humanity to perform most tasks better, faster and cheaper.

This vision will become a reality in the very near future, but along with the benefits will come significant challenges, for which we must be as prepared as possible. It is therefore essential to raise awareness on understanding the radical changes AI will bring to our lives, such as massive number of job losses to automation and robots, the need for establishing ethical standards for the use of AI and robotics, and psychological effects on humans in the shape of technology addiction, anxiety and loneliness, caused by excessive use of AI.

ARTIFICIAL INTELLIGENCE

A simple way of defining Artificial Intelligence as "using computers to do things that normally require human intelligence" might be transformed into a more accurate definition by simply describing AI as "a system with the ability to learn." That system – usually a software or a computer program - can then use that newly acquired knowledge to make a decision in a new situation; just like humans would do. AI is further defined more scientifically as "theories and developments of computer systems that can perform tasks that require human intelligence, such as visual recognition, speech recognition, decision making and cross-language translation."

The term artificial intelligence was first created in 1956, and the research in this field began at a workshop held on the campus of Dartmouth College in NH, USA. Due to lack of necessary computing power, developments in this field nearly stopped during a difficult phase in the 1970s – known as the "*AI winter*". Today the popularity of AI increased tremendously because of the increase in data volume, advanced algorithms and improvements in computing performance and storage. Artificial intelligence is currently the hottest technology paradigm as a branch of computer science that aims to create intelligent machines. It has become an essential part of the technology industry.

Artificial intelligence is a wide-ranging branch of computer science concerned with building smart machines capable of performing tasks, which typically require human intelligence. There are many factors and reasons for the importance of AI.

At first, AI automates repetitive learning and discovery through data. Instead of automating manual tasks, AI reliably performs frequent, large-scale, computerized tasks without fatigue. For this type of automation, human research is still essential for configuring the system and asking the right questions. But AI is different from hardware-centric robot automation.

Next, AI adds more useful functions to existing products. The combination of automation, conversation platforms, robots and intelligent systems with large amounts of data can improve investment intelligence, security and many security intelligence technologies.

Furthermore, AI has the ability to increasingly analyze data with neural networks that have many hidden layers. The construction of fraud detection systems with five hidden layers was almost impossible a few years ago. All this has changed with incredible computer power and vast amounts of ready-to-be-processed data. To train the deep learning models, enormous amounts of data are needed, as such systems learn directly from the data. The more data is available and entered; the more accurate becomes the input.

And finally, artificial intelligence systems adjust themselves through progressive learning algorithms so that the data can be programmed. AI finds structure and regularities in the data, so the algorithm gets a capacity and becomes a classifier or predictor. Just as the algorithm itself can teach you chess, it can also teach you which product to recommend online. And the models adapt when they receive new data. Relay, for example, is an AI technique that can be used to tailor the model by training and adding data if the first answer is not entirely accurate.

Artificial intelligence is an interdisciplinary science with multiple approaches, but advancements in machine learning and deep learning are creating a paradigm shift in virtually every sector of the tech industry. In the 1950s Alan Turing created the *Turing Test*, which is used to determine the level of intelligence of a computer. At its core, AI is the branch of computer science that aims to answer Turing's question in the affirmative. It is an endeavour to replicate or simulate human intelligence in machines.

Weak AI: Artificial intelligence operates in a limited context and is a simulation of human intelligence. Machines with weak AI are made to respond to specific situations, but they are not capable of think for themselves.

Strong AI: A machine with strong AI is able to think and act just like a human. It is able to learn from experiences. General Artificial Intelligence (AGI) is a general intelligence machine, and this intelligence can be used to solve any problem.

Much of Weak AI – also called Narrow AI - is powered by breakthroughs in machine learning and deep learning. An application of AI gives machines the ability to learn and improve without the help of humans or the need for new programming. Understanding the difference between artificial intelligence, machine learning and deep learning can be confusing. The interconnection of these three systems can be accurately described as "Artificial Intelligence is a set of algorithms and intelligence to try to mimic human intelligence. Machine Learning is one of them, and Deep Learning is one of those Machine Learning techniques."

Currently, AI systems are already integrated into many fields and industries worldwide. In the very near future, applications of AI will spread over all aspects of our daily lives.

ECommerce:
In the early 2000s, if we tend to search a web store for a product while not knowing it's exact name, it usually used to be a challenging task. Nowadays, it is entirely sufficient just to type in any keyword - even remotely associated with the item we are seeking – into a search box, and the search engine immediately lists all possible results associated with the item. It's like as if these search engines browse our minds! During a matter of seconds, we tend to get an inventory of all relevant search results. Associated examples include quickly finding the proper movies on Netflix, or audience targeted automated ads based on earlier visited websites or search results.

Finance:
The use of AI in banking is proliferating. A great deal of banks has already adopted AI-based systems to supply client support, sight anomalies, detect credit card frauds and control the ultra-fast transactions between global stock exchange centres. This

tendency is not limited to the banks in the USA and Europe only. Led by Japan, China and Japan, the Asian banks are about to overtake their Western counterparts.

An associated example is the HDFC Bank of India. HDFC Bank has developed an associate AI-based chatbot referred to as *EVA* (Electronic Virtual Assistant), engineered by Senseforth Technologies. Since its launch, *EVA* has self-addressed over three million client queries, interacted with over 5,000,000 distinctive users, and command over 1,000,000 conversations. *EVA* collects information from thousands of sources and supplies easy-to-understand answers in less than 0.4 seconds.

Healthcare:

The time-consuming tasks, such as analysis of health records, medical literature, and historical trends, are ideally suited to AI tools. IBM's AI assistant *Watson* is specialized in the diagnosis and early detection of cancer. Google's *DeepMind* learned from analyzing over 1 million eye scans on how to identify the early signs of eye disease. Because AI tools can review health records and medical data with so much more speed and accuracy than humans, their use can significantly increase the accuracy, and reduce the likelihood of human error, in diagnostics, treatment plans and overall patient care. Predicted developments in this field include robot-assisted surgery, virtual nursing assistants, and hospital administrative workflow assistance.

Other prominent examples of AI applications already make a difference and generate an impact on the fields of governments, agriculture, self-driving cars, market research, sales and education.

MACHINE LEARNING

Machine Learning (ML) is a subsystem of Artificial Intelligence; it is concerned with helping machines to develop human-like skills. For example, let's suppose you want to buy household electronics, such as a washing machine. If machine learning is involved in this purchasing process, ML would also suggest buying washing powder. The formal definition of machine learning states that "the machine can learn automatically from a given set of data and is then able to make suggestions and predictions."

In today's modern world, we are generating a ton of data every day. The data can be of many forms, like structured data, unstructured data, and data in the form of images. These generated data usually contain several impurities like missing values, a disorder of measurement units, different scales, and many more. To eliminate the impurities and transform the data into a readable form, data preprocessing techniques are used. The ML algorithm then further helps the machine to derive some meaningful information from the data. The Main Concepts of Machine Learning are:

1) Supervised Machine Learning

In supervised ML, a labelled set of data is given to the machine as input, and the machine has to predict the output, or the target variable by using supervised machine learning algorithms. The output can be a single labelled output or multiple outputs.

There are two types of supervised learning, namely regression and classification. The popular algorithms used for supervised learning are *random forest, support vector machine,* and *linear regression.*

2) Unsupervised Machine Learning

Here the input consists of unlabeled data. From that data, the machine has to find a pattern that tells us which data belongs to which category. For example, let's suppose, the machine has a bunch of unlabeled animal images as an input. The unsupervised algorithms learn from those unlabeled images, so whenever there is a new image of an animal, the machine can predict the biological class of that animal.

Unsupervised learning can be further divided into clustering and association problems. The most famous algorithms are *K-means clustering, Apriori association rule,* and *K-nearest neighbours.*

3) Semi-supervised Machine Learning

Semi-supervise leaning is a mixture of supervised and unsupervised learning. In this case, the input for the algorithm is a combination of labelled as well as unlabeled data with a ratio of 40:60.

Semi-supervised learning is better suitable for handling the raw format of real-world data. Since there is no need to spend time and memory capacity to put data in a structured format, using semi-supervised learning, helps saving time, space and money.

Other popular machine learning algorithms are *decision tree, ensemble learning, neural networks, ridge regression, support vector machine, Naive Bayes classifier, Bayesian learning*, and *Agglomerative clustering*.

- ❖ Relation of Machine Learning algorithms with other AI blocks

Machine Learning is also related to other disciplines of AI, such as pattern recognition, information retrieval, text processing, image processing, neural network, data mining, big data. They can also be applied to make predictions.

Machine Learning is closely related to Deep Learning because the basis of convolution neural networks and recurrent neural networks is built on Machine Learning. Data Mining discovers patterns and knowledge, which were previously unknown; and Machine Learning reproduces those already known patterns and knowledge. The large quantity of data generated every single day can only be processed with the use of Big Data tools. The most popular Big Data tools are *apache-spark, hadoop*, and *pyspark*.

- ❖ Real-world applications of ML

Medical Industry:
Machine Learning algorithms are capable of discovering insights from patience's medical data and aid doctors to correctly diagnose diseases of genetical disorders. Some of the examples are brain tumor detection, breast cancer, lung cancer, brain hemorrhage, to set regular checkups and many more. In 2025 the medical industry is expected to expand to a more than US$800 billion industry by using artificial intelligence. Major software-based companies like Google, IBM, Amazon and Facebook are already heavily invested in different areas of medical science.

Agriculture Sector:
The agriculture sector uses Machine Learning to improve the productivity and quality of the crops in the agriculture sector. The wide range of applications covers the whole sector, from farmers to retailers. Farmers can use ML technologies to increase the yields of crops and analyze the needs of the seeds. Retailers can use ML to identify possible pesticides in agricultural products.

Weather forecast:
Weather forecasting uses Machine Learning for being able to make more accurate predictions. With the use of Machine Learning, weather models can eliminate inaccurate predictions, such as overestimated snowfall, more efficiently, and generate precise predictions, for example in determining the strength and the path of hurricanes, as well as a nearly exact spot of expected landfall. The meteorological departments use radar stations and satellites to collect up-to-data data. Big Data and different ML algorithms mine and process the gathered data to come up with updated weather models.

The Finance Industry:
The banking sector uses Machine Learning algorithms for many applications. Like to predict the loan defaulters, giving them credit score based on their financial report. Banks use machine learning while issuing credit cards, giving loans. It can be used to identify essential data insights and prevent fraud. The investment bankers like Morgan Stanley, Goldman Sachs use Machine Learning to make investments on stocks. They have to algorithms that can evaluate the companies based on their key financial figures, predict business prospects, and improve profitability.

Recommendation systems:
Netflix uses machine learning and AI to recommend movies. Amazon uses customer purchase history to recommend products. Similar to YouTube and Google.

Traffic Control Systems:
The traffics control board uses deep learning to detect the license plate and to predict potential problems and keep traffic flowing.

Virtual Personal Assistants:
A virtual assistant is a smart software embedded in Smartphones and other connected devices that acts like a personal assistant by helping you mitigate your many tasks so that you can concentrate on the more essential things. What can the Virtual personal assistant do for you? The list expands as the technology moves forward. The smart assistant can locate information online, organize your calendar and set appointments, display a variety of alerts and reminders, activate apps while you drive, and connect with other smart devices, such as IoT electronics. In the past, virtual assistants were backed by simple programs, capable of basic voice recognition. Nowadays, these assistants run on advanced AI and natural language processing technologies. These enable the assistant to understand natural speech and answer just like a human being. Apple's Siri, Amazon's Alexa, Google's Now and Samsung's Bixby are a portion of the instances of Virtual Personal Assistants that aid us in our daily lives.

Cybersecurity:
Machine Learning without human interference can collect, analyze, and methodize knowledge. Within the scope of cybersecurity, ML helps to analyze previous cyber-attacks, to predict new types of attacks, and to develop advanced defense responses. This approach of automatic cyber weaponry elevates a minimum-skilled cybersecurity force to impenetrable system protection.

NEURAL NETWORKS

Neural networks are a set of algorithms, modeled loosely after the human brain, that are designed to recognize patterns. They interpret sensory data through a kind of machine perception, labelling or clustering raw input. The patterns they recognize are numerical, contained in vectors, into which all real-world data, be it images, sound, text or time series, must be translated. Neural networks help us cluster and classify. You can think of them as a clustering and classification layer on top of the data you store and manage. They help to group unlabeled data according to similarities among the example inputs, and they classify data when they have a labelled dataset to train on. Neural networks can also extract features that are fed to other algorithms for clustering and classification; therefore, one can think of deep neural networks as components of larger Machine Learning applications involving algorithms for reinforcement learning, classification and regression.

The Artificial Neural Network was first proposed in the 1970s by the cognitive psychologist and computer scientist Geoffrey Hinton in his research paper. The Artificial neural network consists of the input layer, hidden layer, and one output layer. Perceptron was first introduced in the 1950s and 1960s by the scientist Frank Rosenblatt, inspired by earlier work by Warren McCulloch and Walter Pitts. Today, it is more common to use other models of artificial neurons in general.

It is somehow similar to the neurons in the human body, but neuron in Deep Learning is replaced by perceptron. A perceptron is a neural network unit (an artificial neuron) that does certain computations to detect features or business intelligence in the input data. A perceptron generates out of several binary inputs one single binary output: the neuron output is 0 or 1 determined by the weighted sum.

For example, let's suppose you like to arrange a birthday party. You might make a decision for throwing the party under three conditions.
1) Is there a proper place to organize the party?
2) Are you getting some help from your friends?
3) How is the weather going to be?
These three conditions can be represented by corresponding input variables as x_1, x_2, and x_3. If $x_1=1$, you have a proper place for the party and $x_1=0$ you don't find a place for the party, $x_2=1$ if you are getting some help from your friends and $x_2=0$ you don't get any help, $x_3=1$ for fair weather, $x_3=0$ for rainy weather.
Now you absolutely want to have the party outside in the garden whether your friends are helping you are not. But the weather matters a lot to you. There is no way to throw the party if the weather is bad. The perceptron can be used to solve the problem. One way to do this is to choose a weight $w_3=6$ for the weather, and $w_2=2$ and $w_3=2$ for the other conditions. The more significant value of w_3 indicates that the weather matters a lot to you, much more than the other conditions.

Let's assume that you choose a threshold of 4 for the perceptron. With these choices, the perceptron implements the desired decision-making model, outputting 1 whenever the weather condition is good, and 0 whenever the weather condition is bad. It makes no difference whether you have a proper place or not, or if your friends are helping you or not. If you choose a low value for threshold, it means you have to satisfy other conditions, as well. Dropping the threshold means you're more willing to throw a party.

- ❖ Gradient descent algorithm

Here is a step-by-step approach for a simplified gradient descent algorithm.

Calculate the slope at the current position.
If the slope is negative, move right.
If the slope is positive, move left. (Repeat until slope == 0)

How much should the ball move at each time step?
The steeper the slope, the farther the ball is from the bottom.
Calculate "slope" at current "x" position.
Change x by the negative of the slope. x = x − slope.
Repeat until the slope is equal to 0.

For positive slopes, we move left by a lot. For negative slopes, we move right by a lot. As we get closer to the bottom, it takes tiny steps until slope equals to zero, at which points it stops. This stopping point is called convergence.

Problems might occur with the gradient descent algorithm when slopes are too big, meaning too steep. The step size is based on the steepness of the slope. If the slope is very steep, then the gradient descent algorithm will overshoot by a lot.

Solution 1: Make slopes smaller, meaning less steep. If the gradients are too big, then make them smaller.

Solution 2: Multiply the slope by a single number between 0 and 1. This fraction is typically a single float, called alpha. This solution prevents an overshoot, and the network converges.

- ❖ Improving the Gradient Descent Algorithm

alpha = 0.1 (or some number between 0 and 1)
Calculate "slope" at current "x" position.
x = x − (alpha*slope) (Repeat until slope == 0)

Due to its complex path, we can't find a global minimum, and we are going to stick with the local minimum. To overcome this problem, we use Multiple Random starting states, which means we randomly place many balls and start optimizing all of them to find the global minimum.

Imagine that we randomly place one hundred balls on a line and start optimizing all of them. They would all end up in only five different-colored mapped out positions. The colored regions represent the domain of each local minimum. For example, if a ball randomly falls within the blue domain, it will converge to the blue minimum. This assumption means that to search the entire space, we only have to find five spaces randomly. This method is far better than pure random searching, which has to randomly try every space, which could easily be millions of places on the line depending on the granularity. When slopes are too small, the solution is to increase the alpha.

A cost function is a measure of *how good* a neural network did concerning its given training sample and the expected output. It also may depend on variables such as weights and biases. A cost function is a single value, not a vector because it rates how good the neural network did as a whole.

A cost function is described in the form: $C(W,B,St,Et)$, where
W is the weight of the neural network,
B is the bias of the neural network,
St is the input of a single training sample,
Et is the desired output of that training sample.

In Backpropagation, the cost function is used to compute the error of our output layer. There is a Famous algorithm called Backpropagation is used for computing the gradient of the cost function.

The algorithm consists of 4 steps:
Step 1 - Feed-forward computation
Step 2 - backpropagation to the output layer
Step 3 - backpropagation to the hidden layer
Step 4 - weight updates

The algorithm is stopped when the value of the error function has become sufficiently small.

Furthermore, the common activation functions are:
- Threshold function
- Sigmoid Function
- Rectifier Function
- Tanh function

❖ The utilization of Artificial Neural Systems

From making vehicles drive self-governing on the streets to creating amazingly reasonable CGI faces, to machine interpretation, to extortion discovery, to guessing our thoughts, to perceiving when a feline is in the nursery and turning on the sprinklers; neural nets are behind huge numbers of the greatest advances in A.I. Extensively, be that as it may, they are intended for spotting designs in the information. Explicit undertakings could incorporate order (characterizing informational collections into predefined classes), grouping (arranging information into various vague classifications), and forecast (utilizing past occasions to figure future ones, similar to the financial exchange or film industry).

Similarly, that we gain as a matter of fact in our lives, neural systems expect information to learn. By and large, the more information that can be tossed at a neural system, the more exact it will turn into. Consider it like an assignment you do again and again. After some time, you progressively get increasingly productive and commit fewer errors.

At the point when analysts or computer scientists set out to prepare a neural system, they ordinarily isolate their information into three sets. First is a preparation set, which enables the system to build up the different loads between its hubs. After this, they calibrate it utilizing an information approval index. At last, they'll utilize a test set to check whether it can effectively transform the contribution to the ideal yield.

On a functional level, one of the more considerable difficulties is the measure of time it takes to prepare systems, which can require a lot of figure control for increasingly complex assignments. The most significant issue, nonetheless, is that neural systems are "secret elements," in which the client bolsters in information and gets answers.

They can tweak the appropriate responses, yet they don't approach the definite basic leadership process. This is an issue various analyst are effectively taking a shot at. However, it will just turn out to be all the more squeezing as artificial neural systems play a greater and greater job in our lives.

- ❖ Areas of Application of Neural Network (ANN)

Followings are a portion of the territories, where ANN is being utilized. It recommends that ANN has an interdisciplinary methodology in its improvement and applications.

Speech Recognition: Speech involves an outstanding job in human-human communication. In this manner, it is normal for individuals to expect discourse interfaces with PCs. In the present time, for correspondence with machines, people still need refined dialects which are hard to learn and utilize. To facilitate this correspondence boundary, a straightforward arrangement could be, correspondence in a communicated in language that is workable for the machine to get it.

Extraordinary advancement has been made in this field, in any case; still, such sorts of frameworks are confronting the issue of restricted jargon or language alongside the issue of retraining of the framework for various speakers in various conditions. ANN is assuming a significant job around there. Following ANNs have been utilized for discourse acknowledgement.

Kohonen self-sorting out element map: The most effective system for this is Kohonen self-organizing highlight map, which has its contribution as small portions of the discourse waveform. It will outline some sort of phonemes as the yield cluster, called include extraction procedure. In the wake of separating the highlights, with the assistance of some acoustic models as back-end handling, it will perceive the expression.

Character Recognition: It is a fascinating issue that falls under the general zone of Pattern Recognition. Numerous neural systems have been produced for programmed acknowledgement of written by hand characters, either letters or digits. Even though back-spread neural systems have a few concealed layers, the example of association starting with one layer then onto the next is limited. So also, recognition likewise has a few shrouded layers, and its preparation is done layer by layer for such sort of uses.

Mark Verification Application: MVA is one of the most valuable approaches to approve and validate an individual in legitimate exchanges. Mark check method is a non-vision-based strategy. For this application, the primary methodology is to remove the component or rather the geometrical list of capabilities speaking to the mark. With these capabilities, we need to prepare the neural systems utilizing a practical neural system calculation. This prepared neural system will order the signature as being certified or produced under the confirmation organize.

Human Face Recognition: It is one of the biometric strategies to distinguish the given face. It is a commonplace assignment due to the portrayal of "non-face" pictures. In any case, if a neural system is all around prepared, at that point, it tends to be partitioned into two classes to be specific pictures having appearances and pictures that don't have faces. Initially, all the information pictures must be preprocessed. At that point, the dimensionality of that picture must be decreased. What's more, finally it must be arranged utilizing neural system preparing calculation. Following neural systems are utilized for preparing purposes with a preprocessed picture - completely associated multilayer feed-forward neural system prepared with the assistance of backpropagation calculation. For dimensionality decrease, Principal Component Analysis (PCA) is utilized.

RECURRENT NEURAL NETWORKS

Recurrent Neural Networks, also known as RNNs, are a class of neural networks that allow previous outputs to be used as inputs while having hidden states. In traditional neural networks, all the inputs and outputs are independent of each other. Still, in cases like when it is required to predict the next word of a sentence, the previous words are required, and hence there is a need to remember the previous words. Thus, RNN came into existence, which solved this issue with the help of a Hidden Layer. The primary and crucial feature of RNN is hidden state, which remembers some information about a sequence. RNN belong to the Deep Learning family. RNN process input sequences, which allows them to be proficient in certain types of analyses like speech and writing.

Have you ever thought why the human brain doesn't think from scratch every single time? Let us take an example; imagine you want to classify what kind of event is happening at every point in a movie. RNN has a "memory" which remembers all information about what has been calculated. It uses the same parameters for each input as it performs the same task on all the inputs or hidden layers to produce the output. This reduces the complexity of parameters, unlike other neural networks. With the help of recurrent neural networks, we can solve this problem.

There are five different types of recurrent neural networks.
1. One to one: Vanilla mode of processing without RNN, from fixed-sized input to fixed-sized output. In this type, we have a single input, and we predict a single output - for example, image classification, i.e. predicting a cat or a dog.
2. One to many: Sequence output (e.g. image captioning takes an image and outputs a sentence of words). According to this type, we have a single input, and we predict a series of outputs.
3. Many to one: Sequence input (e.g. sentiment analysis where a given sentence is classified as expressing positive or negative sentiment). In this mode, we have input like a statement, and we have to predict if it is a spam or not - for example, spam classifier, sentiment analysis and 'yes or no' type questions.
4. Many to many (1): Sequence input and sequence output. RNN are given a continuous input, and it provides a continuous output; for example, machine translation (an RNN reads a sentence in English and then outputs a sentence in Spanish), and video classification.
5. Many to many (2): Synced sequence input and output (e.g. video classification where we wish to label each frame of the video).

There are many applications of the recurrent neural network like Natural language processing, Speech recognition, Music generation, Sentiment classification, DNA Sequence Analysis, Machine Translation, Video activity recognition, Named Activity recognition, coming up with product names in marketing, and many more.

There are two main differences between Convolutional Neural Network and Recurrent Neural Network, namely:

CNN accepts only a fixed size vector as input (for example an image) and produces a fixed-sized vector as output (i.e. probabilities of a different class). At the same time in RNN the API is very flexible. It means that can accept fixed-size input as well as a variable input and output a result of desired size (means variable or fixed size).

CNN performs the mapping using a fixed number of computational steps while in RNN uses the variable no of computational steps.

- ❖ Some problems related to RNN.

To connect long term dependencies. One of the appeals of RNN is that they might be able to connect previous information to the present task when we can use a recurrent neural network.

If the gap between relevant information and the place that is needed to small. If the gap grows, recurrent neural network became unable to connect information, so in that we use LSTM.

- ❖ The advantages of RNN can be listed as follows:

Possibility of processing input of any length
Model size not increasing with the size of the input
Computation takes historical information into account
Weights are shared across time

- ❖ To the drawbacks of RNN count:

Slow computation
The difficulty of accessing information from a long time ago
RNN cannot consider any future input for the current state

DEEP LEARNING

Sometimes, we humans are confused by the application of a certain thing in our lives. But once we know that, we can relate the subject to that particular thing and learn. Neural networks also learn by the same pattern. This characteristic makes it easier for us humans to learn about the neural networks when we know the basics. These basics are the fundamental knowledge about Python coding and libraries for building deep learning based on neural networks.

Deep Learning, currently the most advanced and challenging function of AI, mimics the workings of the human brain in processing data for use in decision making. In other words, deep learning is a machine learning technique that teaches computers to do what comes naturally to humans: learn by example. Compared to traditional Machine Learning, Deep Learning can provide superior accuracy, greater versatility and use of big data.

Deep Learning is already having a significant impact and influence on many applications, enabling products to behave intelligently like humans. Made possible through the introduction of high-performance computers and quantum computing, as well as systems for parallel computing, deep learning has today become a reality. Deep Learning can learn from vast amounts of data that is both unstructured and unlabeled that would typically take humans decades to understand and process. Applications include the fields of image recognition and classification [Deep Learning is a key technology behind driverless cars enabling them to recognize traffic light, or to distinguish other vehicles from billboards], voice recognition [This feature is the key to voice control in consumer devices such as mobile phones, and hands-free speakers.], text analysis [Used for a wide variety of applications, for example surfacing unexpected trends in retention, or finding out what keeps users coming back.], and virtual assistants [Software agents, which can interpret human speech and respond via synthesized voices, such as chatbots.].

In recent years, we have witnessed the development of numerous models and architectures of neural networks, the basic structure on which deep learning is built, which led to the definition of data sets. Deep learning utilizes a hierarchical level of artificial neural networks to carry out the process of machine learning. Our brain contains billions upon billions of neurons, each interconnected to generate trillions of connections. This combination of neurons and the connections between them drives our ability to think and act intellectually, to understand our environment and to make decisions about how we interact with this environment.

The artificial neural networks are built like the human brain, with neuron nodes connected like a web. While traditional programs build analysis with data in a linear way, the hierarchical function of deep learning systems enables machines to process data with a nonlinear approach. In deep learning, a computer model learns to perform classification tasks directly from images, text, or sound.

Deep Learning models can achieve state-of-the-art accuracy, often exceeding human-level performance. Models are trained by using a broad set of labelled data and neural network architectures that contain many layers.

Models used in Deep Learning are based on Deep Neural Networks (DNNs), which in turn can use different architectures, such as Convolutional Neural Networks (CNNs) and Recurrent Neural Networks (RNNs). The choice of which architecture to use depends on the specific application. Not connecting all inputs to all of the neurons in the first layer would be the architecture of a CNN, which is particularly well suited for image recognition and classification. Another variation is to create feedback loops such that the output of neurons in later layers act as inputs to earlier layers. This would be the architecture of an RNN, which makes it possible to incorporate latency, to provide a representation of the time which is not captured by traditional machine learning approaches. RNNs are normally used for text or speech recognition.

On a higher level, any Deep Learning application can be divided into two phases, namely *Training* and *Inference*. Training is the process with which the neural network is trained by providing a real set of data and verifying the output-value predicted by the network. At a practical level, this phase consists of tuning, as accurate as possible, the parameters used by the model. In the case of an image classifier, for example, the network is trained by providing tens of thousands of different images. One of the more significant annoyances in the training process is setting the learning rate. The weights of a neural network with hidden layers are highly interdependent. Approaches with the use of methods like linear regression, loss function, and algorithms like stochastic, batch, and mini-batch gradient descent, are necessary to train neural networks.

Linear regression refers to the task of determining a line of best fit through a set of data points and is a simple predecessor to the more complex nonlinear methods we use to solve neural networks. The loss function, or cost function, is a measure of the amount of error the linear regression makes on a dataset.

Today, many problems in multivariable function optimization, including training neural networks, rely on the very effective algorithm of gradient descent to find a suitable solution much faster than taking random guesses. Gradient descent first starts with a random guess at the parameters. It then figures out which direction the loss function steeps downward the most, and steps slightly in that direction. To put it another way, the gradient descent algorithm determines the amounts to tweak all of the parameters such that the loss function goes down by the most considerable amount. It repeats this process over and over until it is satisfied; it has found the lowest point. Training a neural network is a costly operation from a computational point of view, and for this reason, it's not generally performed on the target system. Instead, it's done offline, using high-performance servers or PCs equipped with multi-threaded Graphic Processing Units (GPUs) enabled for parallel processing.

After completing the training phase, the neural network can be installed in the field to perform the inference process, which is to apply the neural network previously trained to a set of real data to infer a result. For example, as part of an AI for a driverless-car, an image classifier can recognize many categories of everyday objects, pedestrians, animals, traffic signs, and other vehicles.

Additional to Artificial Neural Network and the Recurrent Neural Network, there are other prominent Deep Learning algorithms.

- Convolutional Neural Network (CNN)

The Convolutional neural network is a feed-forward neural network that is used to analyze the image processing in grid-like technology. A convolutional neural network is also known as "ConvNet" in the short term. In the Convolutional neural network, every image is represented in the form of arrays of pixel values.
There are mainly four steps in Convolutional Neural Network Architecture
Step 1 - Convolution Layer
Step 2 - Max Pooling
Step 3 - Flattening
Step 4 - Full Connection

The typical applications of convolutional neural networks include:
Computer vision: CNN has used in doing image processing in computer vision.
Image classification: In this, the output can be a single label classifier or multi-label classifier depends on the training data. For example, we have given a dataset that contains different subtypes of brain hemorrhage images. We have to predict the labels of each of the test images.
Object detection: This feature has a lot of applications like Yolo object detection. CNN looks at the object only once and then detects the image in a rectangle-shaped, single-shot detection, such as, license plate recognition.

- Auto-encoder

Auto encoding is a data compression algorithm where the compression and decompression are two functions. That helps to generate the output; the value of the input is the same as the output.
Auto-encoders are information explicit, which implies that they might have the option to pack information like what they have been prepared on. This is not quite the same as, state, the MPEG-2 Audio Layer III (MP3) pressure calculation, which just holds suppositions about "sound" when all is said in done, however not about explicit sorts of sounds. An autoencoder prepared on pictures of appearances would do a somewhat poor activity of packing pictures of trees, in light of the fact that the highlights it would learn would be face-explicit.
Auto-encoders are lossy, which implies that the decompressed yields will be corrupted contrasted with the first information sources (like MP3 or JPEG pressure). This varies from lossless number juggling pressure.
Auto-encoders are found out naturally from information models, which is a valuable property. It implies that it is anything but difficult to prepare particular cases of the calculation that will perform well on a particular sort of info. It doesn't require any new designing, only fitting the preparing information is required.

Step by step approach to use auto-encoder algorithm:
Step 1 - The input layer contains m rows and n columns corresponding to a dataset.
Step 2 - The first input vector x goes into the network.

Step 3 - The input vector x is encoded into a vector y of lower dimensions by mapping functions (for example, tanh or sigmoid functions).
Step 4 - y is decoded into the output vector z of the same dimensions as x.
Step 5 - Compare the output vector z with the input vector x.
Step 6 - Backpropagate from right to left to adjust the weight accordingly. The learning rate decides how much we have to update the weights.
Step 7 - Repeat steps 1 to 6 and update the weights for each observation.
Step 8 - After finishing the first epoch we redo the epochs. Applications of autoencoders include Anomaly detection, Data denoising (ex. images, audio), Image in-painting, Information retrieval.

- Self-Organizing Maps (SOM)

This algorithm is used for reducing the dimensionality. A multi-dimensional dataset with lots of rows and column is represented in the form of a map. That's why it is called Self Organizing Maps.

It is an unsupervised learning algorithm. In the SOM we follow the principle of topographic map formation which states that *"The spatial location of an output neuron in a topographic map corresponds to a particular domain or feature drawn from the input space."*

❖ Applications of Deep Learning

Real Estate: In the real estate sector, we can use neural networks to predict the house price based on the several input parameters like the number of rooms, location (in downtown or in the outskirts of the city), size of land, with or without swimming pool, etc.

Online Advertising: Used to determine whether visitors are clicking the ad or not.

Autonomous driving: This feature uses hybrid Deep Learning algorithms - a combination of a variety of algorithms.

Machine translation: Machine translation can be performed by recurrent RNN, in which user writes a sentence in English and the output results in a French sentence.

Photo tagging: Photo is being tagged by seeing the user face. We use Convolutional neural network to do this.

❖ Boltzmann Machine

A Boltzmann Machine (BM) is a Hopfield net consisting of binary stochastic neurons with hidden units plus the visible units. It is an unsupervised learning algorithm. It is also called as generative learning.

A Restricted Boltzmann Machine (RBM) has the following characteristics:
It contains only two layers.
Visible layers are known as input layers.
Two hidden layers contain hidden variables or latent variables. Latent variables are variables that are not directly observed but instead inferred from other variables that

are observed - for example, football, cricket, outdoor games, tennis, indoor games. Outdoor and indoor are extra pieces of information about football, cricket, and tennis. This type of information is called latent information.

RBM is an asymmetrical bipartite graph, i.e. each node of the visible layer is connected to all node of hidden variables. All the edges are bidirectional or unidirectional. There is no connection between the visible layer and the hidden layer. These are the restriction. Due to this restriction, we could run many algorithms like Gradient-based contrastive divergence; it is also useful in Deep Learning architecture like Deep Belief Network (DBN).

To feed input to the Boltzmann machine, one-hot encoding is used. Defining it for all-out factors where no such ordinal relationship exists, the whole number encoding is simply not sufficient. Utilizing this encoding and enabling the model to expect a characteristic requesting between classes may bring about lackluster showing or surprising outcomes - expectations somewhere between classifications. For this situation, a one-hot encoding can be applied to the whole number portrayal.

RBM can be used in the classification of the image, XML data, and text.
Imbalanced data problems: One class dominates another in the training data.
Noisy labels problem: In some of the examples, training data have different labels.
Missing values issue: Values of some features are unknown.
Unstructured data: The data is represented in unprocessed form like image, videos, document, XML structures.

TENSORFLOW

TensorFlow is a Deep Learning library developed by Google to accelerate Machine Learning and deep neural network research. Google products use machine learning in all of its products to improve the search engine, translation, image captioning or recommendations. Since TensorFlow is capable of running on multiple CPUs, GPUs, and mobile operating systems, it enables data scientists, programmers, and researchers to use the same library to collaborate efficiently.

TensorFlow architecture is designed to work in three parts, namely: (i) pre-process the data, (ii) build the model, (iii) train and estimate the model. In TensorFlow, the input data is represented in the form of a tensor. Tensors are multidimensional arrays an extension of 2D matrices to data with higher dimensions. It is organized according to ranks. Rank 0 means scalar, rank 1 means vector, rank 2 means matrices, rank 3 means 3D tensors like a cube; n^{th} rank means n^{th} tensor. The input goes in at one end, and then it *flows* through the system of multiple operations and comes out the other end as output, hence the name TensorFlow.

The components of TensorFlow are the *tensors* and the *graphs*. The tensor, as the core framework, represents all data types, and it is either a vector or a matrix of multiple dimensions. The graph is an array of successively performed computations. Each operation is called an *op mode,* and they are connected to each other. The graph outlines the ops and connections between the nodes, but it does not display the values. The edge of the nodes is the tensor, which is a way to assign the operation with data.

In TensorFlow there is no need to specify the tensor data type, and the computation is approached as a dataflow graph. It is used to implement the deep neural network. Any TensorFlow code must contain two functions. The first one is building a computational graph, and the second one is running a computational graph. A computational graph is a series of tensor flow operations arranges into a graph of nodes. There is also a tensor board used to visualize the graph on localhost. There are four main tensors: SparseTensor, variable, constant, placeholder.

 # Import tf
With Python, it is a common practice to use a short name for a library to avoid to type the full name of the library. Here we import tensorFlow as tf.
import tensorflow as tf

tf.SparseTensor
TensorFlow represents a sparse tensor as three separate dense tensors: indices, values, and shape. In Python, the three tensors are collected into a SparseTensor class for ease of use.
v = tf.SparseTensor(indices=indices, values=values, shape=shape)

tf.variable
To make the models trainable, we need to be able to modify the graph to get new input. Variables allow us to add a trainable parameter as a graph.
w = tf.Variables([3],tf.float32)

tf.constant
It takes no input and output a value it stores normally.
node = tf.constant(4.0)

tf.placeholder
Accepts the input that is entered by the user.
a = tf.placeholder(tf.float32)

Code examples for implementing a simple TensorFlow model:

```
# Import
import tensorflow as tf
import numpy
import matplotlib.pyplot as plt
learning_rate = 0.01
training_epochs = 1000
display_step = 50

# Training Data
train_X = numpy.asarray([3.3,4.4,5.5,6.71,6.93,4.168,9.779,6.182,7.59,2])
train_Y = numpy.asarray([1.7,2.76,2.09,3.19,1.694,1.573,3.366,2.596,2.53])
n_samples = train_X.shape[0]

# tf Graph Input
X = tf.placeholder("float")
Y = tf.placeholder("float")

# Set model weights
W = tf.Variable(rng.randn(), name="weight")
b = tf.Variable(rng.randn(), name="bias")

# Construct a linear model
pred = tf.add(tf.multiply(X, W), b)

# Mean squared error
cost = tf.reduce_sum(tf.pow(pred-Y, 2))/(2*n_samples)

# Gradient descent
optimizer = tf.train.GradientDescentOptimizer(learning_rate).minimize(cost)

#Graphic display
plt.plot(train_X, train_Y, 'ro', label='Original data')
plt.plot(train_X, sess.run(W) * train_X + sess.run(b), label='Fitted line')
plt.legend()
plt.show()
```

TensorFlow example

TensorFlow incorporates several Application Programming Interfaces (API) to build deep learning architectures like CNN and RNN, and it also supports the

following key algorithms:
Booster tree regression: *tf.estimator.BoostedTreesRegressor*
Boosted tree classification: *tf.estimator.BoostedTreesClassifier*
Classification: *tf.estimator.LinearClassifier*
Deep Learning classification: *tf.estimator.DNNClassifier*
Deep Learning wipe and deep: *tf.estimator.DNNLinearCombinedClassifier*
Linear regression: *tf.estimator.LinearRegressor*

The efficiency of a TensorFlow model can be increased in four steps:
Step 1- Initialize models,
Step 2- Calculate loss by using gradient descent optimizer,
Step 3- Update the variables,
Step 4- Repeat the process until the loss becomes minimal.

Some of the prominent applications of TensorFlow include:
Deep Speech, developed by Mozilla, is a Speech-To-Text engine
Rank Brain, developed by Google, provides more relevant search results for users
Inception Image Classifier, developed by Google, classifies images across
Massive Multitask, developed by Stanford University, is a deep neural network model for identifying promising drug candidates
On Device Computer Vision for Optical Character Recognition (OCR), enables real-time translation.

REINFORCEMENT LEARNING

In Reinforcement learning an AI learns how to optimally interact with the environment using time-delayed labels called rewards as a signal. For example, A five-years old child gets a reward from her teacher if she completes the homework else; she gets punishment from the teacher - as simple as that. The Markov decision process is a mathematical framework for defining the reinforcement learning problem using states, action, and rewards. Though interacting with the environment, an AI will learn a policy which will return an action for a given state with the highest reward. According to the typical framing of a Reinforcement Learning scenario, an agent takes actions in an environment, which is interpreted into a reward and a representation of the state, which are fed back into the agent.

❖ Key terms of Reinforcement Learning

State – it means the agent that is in the present condition in the environment.
Action – the input the agents provide to the environment, calculated by applying a policy to the current state.
Reward – It is a signal from the environment reflecting how well the agent is performing the goals of the game.
Policy – It is mapping from state to action. It is denoted as pi.
Goals – Given the current state, we are in choosing the optimal action which will maximize the long-term expected reward provided by the environment.
Reinforcement learning aims to solve the problems of learning in an environment through trial and error.

There are two types of policy:
- Deterministic Policy
In this type of policy, the actions entirely depend on the input we provide. In mathematical term, we can say that it is a mapping of state to action.
- Stochastic Policy
In this type of policy let the agent choose its action randomly in mathematical Terms. *pi: State * Action* depends upon the probability.

❖ Characteristics and Types of Reinforcement Learning:

The significant attributes are:
There is no boss, just a genuine number or a reward signal.
Consecutive basic leadership.
Time assumes a critical job in Reinforcement issues.
Input is constantly deferred, not prompt.
Specialist's activities decide the consequent information it gets.

Types of Reinforcement Learning are positive and negative.

Positive: It is characterized as an occasion that happens in light of explicit conduct. It builds the quality and the recurrence of the conduct and effects decidedly on the move made by the specialist. This sort of Reinforcement encourages you to amplify execution and continue to change for an increasingly broadened period. Nonetheless, an excessive amount of Reinforcement may prompt over-improvement of state, which can influence the outcomes.

Negative: Negative Reinforcement is characterized as fortifying of conduct that happens as a result of a negative condition that ought to have halted or maintained a strategic distance from. It causes you to characterize the base remain of execution. In any case, the downside of this technique is that it gives enough to get together the base conduct.

❖ Applications of Reinforcement Learning

Assembling

In Fanuc, a robot utilizes profound fortification, figuring out how to pick a gadget from one box and placing it in a holder. Regardless of whether it succeeds or comes up short, it retains the article and gains information and train's it to carry out this responsibility with extraordinary speed and exactness. Many warehousing offices utilized by eCommerce destinations.

And different general stores utilize these canny robots for arranging they're a great many items regular and conveying the correct items to the perfect individuals. If you take a gander at Tesla's production line, it contains more than 160 different types of robots that do a significant piece of work on the electrical cars to lessen the danger of any imperfection.

Stock Management

A significant issue in-store network stock administration is the coordination of stock approaches received by various production network entertainers, for example, providers, makers, wholesalers, to smooth material stream and limit costs while responsively fulfilling client needs.

Support learning calculations can be worked to diminish travel time for stocking just as recovering items in the distribution center for improving space usage and stockroom tasks.

Conveyance Management

Support learning is utilized to tackle the issue of Split Delivery Vehicle Routing. Q-learning is utilized to serve suitable clients with only one vehicle.

Power Systems

Support Learning and streamlining strategies are used to survey the security of the electric power frameworks and to upgrade Micro grid execution. Versatile learning techniques are utilized to create control and assurance plans. Transmission advancements with High-Voltage Direct Current (HVDC) and Flexible Alternating Current Transmission System gadgets (FACTS) in view of versatile learning strategies can adequately diminish transmission misfortunes and CO_2 discharges. Utilizations of Reinforcement Learning are featured for three research issues in control frameworks. To begin with, Reinforcement Learning is utilized to create conveyed control structure for a lot of circulated age sources. The trading of data between these sources is administered by a correspondence chart topology.

Second, an online versatile learning procedure is utilized to control the voltage level of a self-governing Microgrid. The control methodology is robust against any unsettling influences in the states and burden. Just fractional information about the Microgrid's elements is required. At long last, Q-Learning with 'qualification follows strategy' is embraced to tackle the power frameworks non-curved Economic Dispatch issue with valve point stacking impacts, different fuel choices, and power transmission misfortunes. The 'qualification follows' are utilized to accelerate the Q-Learning process.

Fund Sector

Pit.AI is at the bleeding edge utilizing support learning for assessing exchanging methodologies. It is ending up being a vigorous device for preparing frameworks to improve monetary goals. It has massive applications in financial exchange exchanging where Q-Learning calculation can get familiar with an ideal exchanging methodology with one basic guidance; amplify the estimation of our portfolio.

Thusly any individual who can get his/her hands on a Q-Learning calculation will possibly have the option to pick up pay with agonizing over the market cost or the dangers required since the Q-Learning calculation is savvy to take all these under contemplations while making an exchange.

The prime purposes behind utilizing Reinforcement Learning are the fact that it encourages you to discover which circumstance needs an activity. It further encourages you to find which activity yields the most elevated reward over the more drawn out period. Support Learning additionally furnishes the learning specialist with reward work. It additionally enables it to make sense of the best strategy for acquiring enormous prizes.

❖ Difficulties of Reinforcement Learning

You have to recollect that processing with Reinforcement Learning can be overwhelming and tedious. Specifically, when the activity space is enormous. Here are the significant difficulties you will confront while doing Reinforcement Acquiring:

Highlight/remunerate plan which ought to be extremely included
Parameters may influence the speed of learning.
Reasonable conditions can have incomplete discernibleness.
An excessive amount of Reinforcement may prompt an over-burden of states which can reduce the outcomes.
Reasonable situations can be non-stationary.

Q-LEARNING

Quality-Learning, or Q-Learning is a model-free type of Reinforcement Learning algorithm that seeks the best action to take given the current state. AS described in the previous chapter, Reinforcement Learning briefly is a paradigm of a learning process in which a learning agent learns, over time, to behave optimally in a certain environment by interacting continuously in the environment. The agent, during its course of learning, experiences various different situations in the environment it is in. These are called states. The agent, while being in that state, may choose from a set of allowable actions which may fetch different rewards. The learning agent overtime learns to maximize these rewards to behave optimally at any given state it is in.

Q-Learning is a basic form of Reinforcement Learning which uses Q-values to improve the behavior of the learning agent iteratively. Quality, in this case, represents how useful a given action is in gaining some future reward. Q-learning is an off-policy reinforcement learning algorithm that seeks to find the best action to take given the current state. It's considered off-policy because the Q-learning function learns from actions that are outside the current policy, like taking random actions, and therefore policy isn't needed. Q-learning seeks to learn a policy that maximizes the total reward. The various applications of Q-Learning include stock trading, sports betting, internet of things, and many more.

The key phrases of Q-learning are:
(1) Learn implies that we are not supposed to hand-code any particular strategy, but the algorithm should learn by itself.
(2) Policy is the result of the learning. Given a state of the environment, the Policy will tell us how best to interact with it so as to maximize the Rewards.
(3) Interact is nothing but the "Actions" the algorithm should recommend us to take under different circumstances.
(4) Environment is the black box the algorithm interacts with. It is the game it is supposed to win. It's the world we live in. It's the universe and all the suns and the stars and everything else that can influence the environment and its reaction to the action taken.
(5) Circumstances are the different "States" the environment can be in.
(6) Reward is the goal. It's the purpose of interacting with the environment and the purpose of playing the game.

When Q-learning is performed, a Q-table or Q-matrix is created that follows the shape of [state, action]; the values are initialized to zero. After each episode, the Q-values are updated and stored.
Hence, the Q-table becomes a reference table for the agent to select the best action based on the Q-value.

```
import numpy as np
# Initialize q-table values to 0
Q = np.zeros((state_size, action_size))
```

The next step is for the agent to interact with the environment and make updates to the state-action pairs in the Q-table. *Q[state, action]*

An agent interacts with the environment in one of two ways, namely either by using the Q-table as a reference or by taking actions randomly. According to the first method of interaction with the environment, the agent views all possible actions for a given state. The agent then selects the action based on the max value of those actions. This is known as exploiting since the available information is used to make a decision.

The second random method is called exploring. Instead of selecting actions based on the max future reward, the agent selects an action at random. Acting randomly is important because it allows the agent to explore and discover new states that otherwise may not be selected during the exploitation process. Exploration and exploitation can be balanced by using epsilon (ε) and setting the value of how often you want to explore vs exploit. Here's a basic code sample that will depend on how the state and action space are setup.

```
import random
# Set the percent you want to explore
epsilon = 0.2
if random.uniform(0, 1) < epsilon:
    """
    Explore: select a random action
    """
else:
    """
    Exploit: select the action with max value (future reward)
    """
```

Updating the Q-table occurs after each step or action and ends when an episode is done. Done in this case means reaching some terminal point by the agent. A final state, for example, can be anything like landing on a checkout page, reaching the end of some game, completing some desired objective. The agent will not learn much after a single episode, but eventually, with enough exploring (steps and episodes) it will converge and learn the optimal Q-values or Q-star (Q*). The performed three basic states are, therefore: 1) Agent starts in a state (s_1), takes an action (a_1), and receives a reward (r_1). 2) Agent selects action by referencing Q-table with the highest value (max) or by random (epsilon, ε). 3) The update of the Q-values.

The Q-values are adjusted based on the difference between the discounted new values and old values. The new values are discounted using the gamma, and the step size is adjusted using the learning rate.

```
# Update Q values
Q[state, action] = Q[state, action] + lr * (reward + gamma * np.max(Q[new_state, :]) - Q[state, action])
```

The variables used in the above-shown code sequence are:

Learning Rate: *lr*, often referred to as *alpha* or α, can simply be defined as how much you accept the new value to change versus the old value. Above we are taking the difference between new and old and then multiplying that value by the learning rate. This value then gets added to our previous Q-value, which essentially moves it in the direction of our latest update.

Gamma: gamma or γ is a discount factor. It's used to balance immediate and future reward. From our update rule above, you can see that we apply the discount to the future reward. Typically, this value can range anywhere from 0.8 to 0.99.

Reward: reward is the value received after completing a specific action at a given state. A reward can happen at any given time step or only at the final time step.

Max: *np.max()* uses the NumPy library and is taking the maximum of the future reward and applying it to the reward for the current state. What this does is impact the current action by the possible future reward. This is the main advantage of Q-learning. We're allocating future reward to current actions to help the agent select the highest return action at any given state.

DATA MINING

The numbers are staggering! The quantity of data created is doubling every two years; we have generated 99% of data in just four to five years. Some sources generate tons of data in sensor form, and these large data quantities can only be handled through the use of Big Data tools. Unstructured data alone makes up 90% of the digital universe. However, additional information does not necessarily mean additional data, because real-world data is usually available in a messy, unstructured, and unlabeled form.

Data mining is the exploration and analysis of extensive data to discover meaningful patterns and rules. It's considered a discipline under the data science field of study and differs from predictive analytics because it describes historical data, while data mining aims to predict future outcomes. Additionally, data mining techniques are used to build Machine Learning models that power advanced Artificial Intelligence applications such as search engine algorithms and recommendation systems. The field of data mining is created to generate meaningful insights from the data and make them available in a proper readable form.

Data mining is the process of finding anomalies, patterns and correlations at intervals giant information sets to predict outcomes. Using a broad variation of techniques, AI algorithms and applications can further use the mined big data to perform the tasks they are designed for. The main task of data mining is to remove all the anomalies which might be hidden in the information. In other words: understand what's relevant then observe the use of that information to assess doubtless outcomes.

Data mining techniques are broadly classified into two types, namely, supervised and unsupervised learning. In the case of supervised learning, the machine already has labelled data as input, while in unsupervised learning, there are no specific labels assigned to the data. The machine just learns from the vast amount of data assigned to a class.

While you can use each approach independently, it is quite common to use both during an analysis. Each approach has unique advantages and combines to increase the robustness, stability, and overall utility of data mining models. The goal of supervised learning is prediction or classification. Unsupervised tasks focus on understanding and describing data to reveal underlying patterns within it. Supervised models can benefit from nesting variables derived from unsupervised methods. For example, a cluster variable within a regression model allows analysts to eliminate redundant variables from the model and improve its accuracy.

Because unsupervised approaches reveal the underlying relationships within data, analysts should use the insights from unsupervised learning to springboard their supervised analysis.

❖ Main Concepts and Algorithms in Data Mining

1) Clustering
It is an unsupervised learning technique that represents natural groups in your data. It clusters similar items together. There are two main algorithms in this. The first one is *K-means clustering*, and another one is *Agglomerative clustering*. In *K-means clustering*, we group the data by using Euclidean distance formula. It uses an iterative approach to form clusters. In *Agglomerative clustering*, there are two approaches top-down and bottom-up.

2) Association rule
Association rule discovery is to find relationships between different items in the database. It is usually expressed in the form X => Y. Where X and Y are sets of properties in the dataset that mean that the transaction involving X also includes Y. There are some types of Association rules. *Apriori* algorithm is also called a recommendation algorithm. Netflix uses the *Apriori* algorithm to recommend movies to the customer. It uses the support and confidence rule to do this.

3) Classification
Classification is a supervised learning method. How to classify or assign class labels to pattern sets under supervision. The purpose of the classification is to develop a model for each class. The classification method is based on the following algorithms:

K-nearest neighbors: An object is classified by a majority vote of its neighbors, with the object being assigned to the class most common among its *k-nearest neighbors*. It can also be used for the regression target is the value for the object (which predicts continuous values). This value is the average (or median) of the values of its *k-nearest neighbors* that help in prediction. For a new data point, it measures the Euclidean distance between two class and predicts the category of that neighbors.

Naive Bayes classifier: It uses Bayes theorem to classify the data points based on their probability. The proper definition is *Naive Bayes classifiers* are a gathering of characterization calculations dependent on Bayes' Theorem. It's anything but a solitary calculation yet a group of calculations where every one of them shares a typical rule; for example, each pair of highlights being grouped is autonomous of one another.

Decision tree classifier: It is having a tree-like structure having certain code sequences embedded in it. It is one of the most widely used classification methods as it is easy to interpret and can be expressed under if-then-else rule conditions.

Random forest classifier: This is a combination of decision tree algorithms. It is also called ensemble learning, which means a combination of different algorithms to make something compelling.

4) Statistical regression
The most commonly used regression techniques are *Linear regression*. In linear regression, the output is dependent on the single input variable.
The mathematical notation is $y = mx + b$. Where y is the output variable, x is input variable, m is regressor coefficients, and b is biased (noise that is adding to the data). There are also other types of regression like *Multiple regression*, *Polynomial regression*, *Ridge regression*, *Lasso regression* and *Elastic net regression*.

❖ Data Mining/Processing Applications and Trends

Data Processing is employed for analysis, for monetary estimation programs, for instructional functions, for dominant area trade vehicles, like rockets or, lunar landing machines. It is additionally utilized in the insurance trade. Some more applications like in automated banking algorithms help banks understand their customer base as well as the billions of transactions at the heart of the financial system.

Data Mining helps money services firms get an improved read of market risks, discover fraud quicker, manage regulative compliance obligations and obtain optimum returns on their selling investments. And in the retail industry, large customer databases hold hidden customer insight that can help you improve relationships, optimize marketing campaigns and forecast sales. It means more accurate data models; retail companies can offer more targeted campaigns, and find a discount that makes the most significant impact on the customer.

- Language Standardization

Similar to the way that SQL evolved to become the preeminent language for databases, users are beginning to demand a standardization among data mining. This push allows users to conveniently interact with many different mining platforms while only learning one standard language. While developers are hesitant to make this change, as more users continue to support it, we can expect a standard language to be developed within the next few years.

- Scientific Mining

With its proven success in the business world, data mining is being implemented in scientific and academic research. Psychologists now use association analysis to track and identify broader patterns in human behavior to support their research. Economists similarly employ forecasting algorithms to predict future market changes based on present-day variables.

- Complex Data Objects

As data mining expands to influence other departments and fields, new methods are being developed to analyze increasingly varied and complex data. Google experimented with a visual search tool, whereby users can conduct a search using a picture as input in place of text. Data mining tools can no longer just accommodate text and numbers; they must have the capacity to process and analyze a variety of complex data types.

- Increased Computing Speed

As data size, complexity, and variety increase, data mining tools require faster computers and more efficient methods of analyzing data. Each new observation adds a new computation cycle to an analysis. As the quantity of data increases exponentially, so do the number of cycles needed to process the data. Statistical techniques, such as clustering, were built to handle a few thousand observations with a dozen variables efficiently. However, with organizations collecting millions of new observations with hundreds of variables, the calculations can become too complex for many computers to handle. As the size of data continues to grow, faster computers and more efficient methods are needed to match the required computing power for analysis.

- Web mining

With the expansion of the internet, uncovering patterns and trends in usage is an excellent value to organizations. Web mining uses the same techniques like data mining and applies them directly on the internet. The three major types of web mining are content mining, structure mining, and usage mining. Online retailers, such as Amazon, use web mining to understand how customers navigate their webpage. These insights allow Amazon to restructure its platform to improve customer experience and increase purchases.

BIG DATA

Big Data is a field that treats approaches to investigate, methodically separate data from, or generally manage informational collections that are too huge or complex to be managed by customary information handling application programming. Information with numerous cases (lines) offers more prominent factual power, while information with higher intricacy (more properties or sections) may prompt a higher false disclosure rate.

Enormous information difficulties incorporate catching information, information stockpiling, information investigation, searching, sharing, moving, perception, and questioning, refreshing, data protection and information source. Vast information was initially connected with three key ideas: volume, assortment, and speed. At the point when we handle enormous information, we may not test; however, basically, watch and track what occurs. In this way, huge information regularly incorporates information with sizes that surpass the limit of conventional standard programming to process inside an adequate time and worth.

❖ Characteristics of Big Data

1) Volume
As we know, we are generating trillions of data every year. A text file is consisting of few kilobytes, whereas a sound file is a few megabytes while a full-length movie is a few gigabytes. Google handles more than 20 million customers every day on the Google platform. The large volume of data is a major characteristic of big data.

2) Speed
Speed measures how fast data is produced and modified and the speed with which it needs to be processed; even the supercomputer processes the data in petaflops. As the increasing products of IoT devices Stream the data at a very high speed. For example- 72 hours of video are uploaded to YouTube every minute; this is the velocity. Extremely high speed of data is another significant data characteristic.

3) Variety
In today's world data is present in many forms like structured data, unstructured data, semi-structured data.

Structured data
It is found in the form of tables consists of row and column. It has a very well-defined meaning. The intersection of the line and the segment in a cell has a worth and is given a "key," which is very well may be alluded to in inquiries. Since there is an immediate connection between the section and the column, these databases are generally alluded to as social databases.

For example - a database that consists of name, branch, and country.

Name	Branch	Country
Stuart	Mechanical	Australia
Lee Sheng	Mechanical	China
Sam	Agriculture	USA
Alisha	CSE	India
Nakamura	CSE	Japan

Semi-Structured data
It is not in the form of table structure because it is more readable in XML form.
    For example, XML data:
<student>
<name>Lee Sheng </name>
<branch>CSE</branch>
</student>

Unstructured data
The data is in the form of audio, video, images, text or we can say that any data which is not in the form of tables. In real-world 90% of our data is in an unstructured format. For example, the output returned by Google search, raw images, corpora of text files, uncensored images and many more.

- ❖ The main applications and users of Big Data:

1) Banking and Securities Industry
The Securities Exchange Commission (SEC) is utilizing vast information to screen monetary market action. They are right now utilizing system investigation and regular language processors to get illicit exchanging action the budgetary markets.
Retail dealers, Big banks, speculative stock investments, and other purported 'enormous young men's in the money related markets utilize huge information for exchange examination utilized in high-recurrence exchanging, pre-exchange choice help investigation, conclusion estimation, Predictive Analytics, and so on.
This industry likewise vigorously depends on an enormous amount of information for chance examination, including; hostile to illegal tax avoidance, request undertaking hazards the board, "Know Your Customer," and extortion moderation.

2) Communication, Media and Entertainment Industry
Associations in this industry all the while examining client information alongside conduct information to make the point by point client profiles that can be utilized to:
Make content for various objective spectators
Suggest content on request.
Measure content execution.
Spotify, an on-request music administration, utilizes Hadoop enormous information examination, to gather information from its a large number of clients worldwide and afterwards utilizes the broke down information to give educated music proposals to singular clients.

Amazon Prime, which is headed to give an extraordinary client experience by offering video, music, and Kindle books in a one-stop-shop, additionally vigorously uses enormous information.

Enormous Data Providers in this industry incorporate Info chimps, Splunk, Pervasive Software, and Visible Measures.

3) Health care

The social insurance part approaches enormous measures of information yet has been tormented by disappointments in using the information to check the expense of rising human services and by wasteful frameworks that smother quicker and better medicinal services advantages no matter how you look at it.

This is for the most part on the grounds that electronic information is inaccessible, insufficient, or unusable. Moreover, the social insurance databases that hold wellbeing related data have made it hard to connect information that can show designs valuable in the medicinal field.

4) Education

Enormous information is utilized primarily in advanced education. For instance, The University of Tasmania. An Australian college with more than 26000 understudies has sent a Learning and Management System that tracks, in addition to other things, when an understudy sign onto the framework, how much time is spent on various pages in the framework, just as the general advancement of an understudy after some time.

In an alternate use instance of the utilization of enormous information in training, it is likewise used to quantify an educator's viability to guarantee an excellent encounter for the two understudies and instructors. Instructor's exhibition can be adjusted and estimated against understudy numbers, topic, understudy socioeconomics, understudy desires, conduct arrangement, and a few other variables.

5) Government sector

Government is a relevant field that is strongly impacted by AI technologies, especially by Big Data. In public services, big data has an extensive range of applications, including energy exploration, financial market analysis, fraud detection, health-related research, and environmental protection.

Big data is being used in the analysis of large amounts of social disability claims made to the Social Security Administration (SSA) that arrive in the form of unstructured data.

Public Safety and Security: Big data can provide customized reports of potential locations and windows of time in which crime is more likely to occur. Another AI feature is biometric facial recognition technology. Concerns about these applications are raised because they may lead to racial profiling and bias against minorities.

Bureaucratic Efficiency: Government workers can save vast amounts of time by automating simple, repetitive tasks. Implementing AI solutions can save $billions in staff-hours annually. In countries, such as Canada, the UK, China and Finland, have assembled specific committees and research groups to provide consulting services and recommendations to those governments regarding the growth of AI and how their countries could benefit from it.

❖ Relation of Big Data with other AI blocks

Big Data and AI are viewed as two mechanical mammoths by information researchers or other huge organizations. Numerous associations think about what AI will acquire the unrest in their hierarchical information. AI is considered as a propelled adaptation of AI through which different machines can send or get information and adopt new ideas by dissecting the information.

Enormous information helps the associations in investigating their current information and in drawing essential bits of knowledge from the equivalent. Here, for instance, we can consider a calfskin article of clothing producer that fares its pieces of clothing to the European and don't have any thought regarding the client premiums than just by gathering information from the market and breaking down it through different calculations, the dealer can recognize the client conduct and premiums. According to their inclinations, they can give the materials.

For this, the calculations can discover knowledge and precise data as well. So in this way, unmistakably the converge of AI and Big Data can't just include the ability and adapting all the while, yet in addition offer ascent to numerous new ideas and choices for any new brand and association. A blend of AI and Big Data can assist the associations with knowing the client's enthusiasm for an ideal way. By utilizing AI ideas, the associations can distinguish the client's advantages in the least conceivable time.

❖ The following AI advances are utilized with Big Data:

Anomaly Detection
For any dataset, on the off chance that an abnormality isn't distinguished, at that point Big Data investigation can be utilized. Here flaw identification, sensor organize, eco-framework conveyance framework wellbeing can be distinguished with enormous information advances.

Bayes Theorem
Bayes's hypothesis is utilized to recognize the likelihood of an occasion dependent on the pre-known conditions. Indeed, even the fate of any occasion can likewise be anticipated based on the past occasion. For Big Data investigation, this hypothesis is of best use and can give a probability of any client enthusiasm for the item by utilizing the past or verifiable information example.

Pattern Recognition
Pattern Recognition is a system of AI and is utilized to distinguish the examples in a specific measure of information. With the assistance of preparing information, the examples can be distinguished and are known as regulated or supervised learning.

Graph Theory
The graph hypothesis depends on the chart study that utilizations different vertices and edges. Through hub connections, the information example and relationship can be distinguished. This example can be valuable and help information experts in design distinguishing proof. This investigation can be significant and valuable for any business.

CONCLUSIONS

The author hopes that after reading this book, you now have an overall understanding of what machine learning, deep learning, big data, neural networks, and artificial intelligence are, why they are essential, how they work and interact with each other.

This book began its examination of AI, by defining the terms, giving you the data definitions needed to understand the elements at play. AI is a difficult quality to really get a grasp of because it can be something as simple as an algorithm that teaches a device to recognize a pedestrian at a zebra crossing, or it can be something that a business installs on their servers that analyzes structured data and makes predictions and recommendations about global financial trends.

The author wishes to underline the fact, that while components of AI are mainly mathematically based topics, they can only realize their full potential when they are implemented with related business, social, ethical, political and legal aspects taken into consideration. What makes artificial intelligence unique is the tenuous and continuously changing relationship that exists between AI and life.

It is therefore vital to recognize the significant challenge the growth of AI will bring to our lives in the very near future and tackle them proactively. Let artificial intelligence assist you in your life, but don't let it take over or *become* your life.

Appendix

Installation of Anaconda on Windows, Linux, and MacOS

1) Installing Anaconda on Windows
Visit https://Anaconda.com/downloads
Select Windows
Download the .exe installer
Open and run the .exe installer
Open the Anaconda Prompt and run some Python code

2) Installing Anaconda on Linux
Visit https://Anaconda.com/downloads
Select Linux
Copy the bash (.sh file) installer link
Use wget to download the bash installer
Run the bash script to install Anaconda3
source the .bash-rc file to add Anaconda to your PATH
Start the Python REPL

3) Installing Anaconda on MacOS
Visit https://Anaconda.com/downloads
Select MacOS and Download the .pkg installer
Open the .pkg installer
Follow the installation instructions
Source your .bash-rc file
Open a terminal and type python and run some code.

ABOUT THE AUTHOR

Marc Stanford holds a Master's degree in Advanced Computer Science and currently works on his Doctoral Thesis on Neural Networks. In his professional career, he is specialized, among others, in artificial intelligence, and complex data modeling.

Although already experienced in tutoring and lecturing, writing books about technical subjects is Marc's newest passion. He lives and works in Palo Alto, CA, USA.

Also, by Marc Stanford

Programming with Python
An Easy to Understand Beginners Guide to Coding with Python

Non-fiction, eBook and paperback published in October 2019, ISBN-13: 9781696419642, available at Amazon in all marketplaces

Ethical Hacking
The Complete Beginners Guide to Basic Security and Penetration Testing

Non-fiction, eBook and paperback published in October 2019, ISBN-13: 9781698148427, available at Amazon in all marketplaces

ECOMMERCE 2020 & BEYOND
Dropshipping, Retail Arbitrage, SEO, Social media Marketing & More

Non-fiction, eBook and paperback published in October 2019, ISBN-13: 9781705601433, available at Amazon in all marketplaces

Printed in Great Britain
by Amazon